The Personal and Intimate Relationship Skills Workbook

Self-Assessments, Exercises & Educational Handouts

Ester A. Leutenberg

John J. Liptak, EdD

Illustrated by

Amy L. Brodsky, LISW-S

Whole Person Associates
Duluth, Minnesota

Whole Person Associates
210 West Michigan Street
Duluth, MN 55802-1908

800-247-6789

books@wholeperson.com
www.wholeperson.com

The Personal and Intimate Relationship Skills Workbook
Self-Assessments, Exercises & Educational Handouts

Printed in the United States of America

10 9 8 7 6 5 4 3 2 1

Editorial Director: Carlene Sippola
Art Director: Joy Morgan Dey

Library of Congress Control Number: 2009941905
ISBN: 978-1-57025-238-9

Using This Book *(For the professional)*

Being in an intimate relationship can be one of the most joyful experiences imaginable. Intimate relationships play a critical role in a person's overall health and wellness. An intimate relationship provides an antidote to the worries, tension, depression and the stress of our everyday lives. Something magical happens when two people connect with each other in an intimate way. Human beings have a universal need to belong and to connect which is satisfied when intimate relationships are formed. Intimate relationships can be the best – and most challenging – part of a person's existence.

Specific signs identified as indications of a healthy relationship

- Respect for each other's privacy
- Communicate in an open, honest and direct way
- Pride in each other's work, accomplishments and successes
- Time together is enjoyable and fun
- Sense of feeling safe with each other
- Trust in each other
- Faithfulness to each other
- Encouragement of each others' interests
- Appreciation of family and friends that are supportive to both partners
- Important matters discussed openly and freely - each has an equal say
- Allowing private space for each other
- Ease in talking to each other about feelings
- Willingness to prioritize each other
- Positive feelings about how one is treated and how each treats the other
- Support of each other's goals
- Acceptance of responsibility for actions
- Willingness to listen and to respect the right for each other
- Apologies sincerely offered when wrong
- Shared decision making
- Awareness of need for alone time
- Affectionate treatment of each other
- Arguments solved without hurting each other
- Respect for each other

Personal, intimate and healthy relationships are full of joy, fun, romance, intense feelings and mutual support. True intimacy requires that people develop empathy, or the ability to consider their partner's point of view. Intimate relationships grow with time, and interestingly enough, the more people get to know themselves, the more empathetic they become and the easier it is to develop healthy relationships. The goal of *The Personal and Intimate Relationship Skills Workbook* is to help each participant explore personal and partner behaviors. This workbook incorporates interesting and eye-opening assessments to encourage each reader to explore personal relationship behavior, as well as that of their partner.

(Continued)

Using This Book *(For the professional, continued)*

The Personal and Intimate Relationship Skills Workbook contains five separate sections to help participants learn more about themselves, and the skills that are fundamental to developing and maintaining healthy relationships. They will discover and better understand the importance of these skills in living in harmony with a relationship partner.

Sections of this book

1) **PARTNER COMMUNICATION SKILLS SCALE** helps each individual explore the effectiveness of existing personal interactions.

2) **PARTNER PERSONALITY SCALE** helps each individual better understand personal personality characteristics as compared to those of a partner.

3) **RELATIONSHIP NEEDS SCALE** helps each individual identify and explore personal dominant needs and the needs of a partner, and then help to determine their compatibility.

4) **RELATIONSHIP INTIMACY SCALE** helps each individual examine the quality of the intimacy in the relationship with a partner.

5) **RELATIONSHIP CONFLICTS SCALE** helps each individual identify the primary issues that cause the most conflict with a partner.

These sections serve as avenues for individual self-reflection, as well as for group experiences revolving around identified topics of importance. Each assessment includes directions for easy administration, scoring and interpretation. Each section includes exploratory activities, reflective journaling activities and educational handouts to help participants discover their habitual effective and ineffective relationship skills and provides instruction for enhancing their most critical partner relationship weaknesses.

The art of self-reflection goes back many centuries and is rooted in many of the world's greatest spiritual and philosophical traditions. Socrates, the ancient Greek philosopher, was known to walk the streets engaging the people he met in philosophical reflection and dialogue. He felt that this type of activity was so important in life that he went so far as to proclaim, "The unexamined life is not worth living!" The unexamined life is one in which the same routine is continually repeated without ever thinking about its meaning to one's life and how this life really could be lived. However, a structured reflection and examination of beliefs, assumptions, characteristics, and patterns can provide a better understanding, which can lead to a more satisfying life. A greater level of self-understanding about important life skills is often necessary to make positive, self-directed changes in the negative patterns that keep repeating. The assessments and exercises in this book can help promote this self-understanding. Through involvement in the in-depth activities, the participant claims ownership in the development of positive patterns.

(Continued)

Using This Book *(For the professional, continued)*

Journaling is an extremely powerful tool for enhancing self-discovery, learning, transcending traditional problems, breaking ineffective life habits, and promote healing from psychological traumas of the past. From a physical point of view, writing reduces stress and lowers muscle tension, blood pressure and heart rate levels.

Psychologically, writing reduces sadness, depression and general anxiety, and leads to a greater level of life satisfaction and optimism. Behaviorally, writing leads to enhanced social skills, emotional intelligence and creativity. It also leads to improved relationship skills, which leads to more self-confidence in personal and intimate relationships.

By combining reflective assessment and journaling, participants will be exposed to a powerful method of combining verbalizing and writing to reflect on and solve problems. Participants will become more aware of the strengths and weaknesses of their specific relationship and relationship-building skills.

Preparation for using the assessments and activities in this book is important. The authors suggest that prior to administering any of the assessments in this book, you complete them yourself. This will familiarize you with the format of the assessments, the scoring directions, the interpretation guides and the journaling activities. Although the assessments are designed to be self-administered, scored and interpreted, this familiarity will help prepare facilitators to answer questions about the assessments for participants.

Participants will be asked to respond based on their current relationship or any relationship from their past. The results will be most effective if they refer to the same relationship situation throughout the book.

The Assessments, Journaling Activities and Educational Handouts

The Assessments, Journaling Activities, and Educational Handouts in *The Personal and Intimate Relationship Skills Workbook* are reproducible and ready to be photocopied for participants' use. Assessments contained in this book focus on self-reported data and are similar to ones used by psychologists, counselors, therapists, and marriage and family therapists. Accuracy and usefulness of the information provided is dependent on the truthful information that each participant provides through self-examination. By being honest, participants help themselves to learn about unproductive and ineffective relationship patterns, and to uncover information that might be keeping them from being as happy and/or as successful in relationships as they might be.

An assessment instrument can provide participants with valuable information about themselves; however, it cannot measure or identify everything about them. The purposes of the assessments are not to pigeon-hole certain characteristics, but rather to allow participants to explore all of their characteristics. This book contains self-assessments, not tests. Tests measure knowledge or whether something is right or wrong. For the assessments in this book, there are no right or wrong answers. These assessments ask for personal opinions or attitudes about a topic of importance in the participant's career and life.

When administering assessments in this workbook, remember that although the items are generically written, so they will be applicable to a wide variety of people, the items will not account for every possible variable for every person. The assessments are not specifically tailored to one specific type of person. They are designed to help participants identify strengths in their personalities and positive behaviors that support and nurture personal and intimate relationships as well as to help participants identify possible negative themes in their lives and find ways to break the hold that these patterns and their effects have.

Advise the participants taking the assessments that they should not spend too much time trying to analyze the content of the questions; their initial response will most likely be true. Regardless of individual scores, encourage participants to talk about their findings and their feelings pertaining to what they have discovered about themselves. Talking about issues encountered in relationships can enhance the overall well-being of participants. These wellness exercises can be used by group facilitators working with any populations who want to strengthen their relationships.

A particular score on any assessment does not guarantee a participant's level of relationship happiness. Use discretion when using any of the information or feedback provided in this workbook. The use of these assessments should not be substituted for consultation and/or counseling from a psychological or medical professional.

Thanks to the following professionals whose input in this book has been so valuable!

Kathy Khalsa, MAJS, OTR/L   Kathy Liptak, Ed.D.

Jay Leutenberg   Eileen Regen, M.Ed., CJE

Layout of the Book

In this book:

- **Assessment Instruments** – Self-assessment inventories with scoring directions and interpretation materials. Group facilitators can choose one or more of the activities relevant to their participants.

- **Activity Handouts** – Practical questions and activities that prompt self-reflection and promote self-understanding. These questions and activities foster introspection and promote pro-social behaviors.

- **Journaling Activities** – Self-exploration activities and journaling exercises specific to each assessment to enhance self-discovery, learning and healing.

- **Educational Handouts** – Handouts designed to supplement instruction can be used individually or in groups. They can be distributed, converted into masters for overheads or transparencies, or written down on a board and discussed.

Who should use this program?

This book has been designed as a practical tool for helping professional therapists, counselors, marriage and family therapists, psychologists, teachers, group leaders, etc. Depending on the role of the professional using *The Personal and Intimate Relationship Skills Workbook* and the specific group's needs, these sections can be used individually, combined, or implemented as part of an integrated curriculum for a more comprehensive approach.

Why use self-assessments?

Self-assessments are important in teaching various life skills.
Participants will:

- Become aware of the primary motivators that guide behavior.

- Explore and learn to indentify potentially harmful situations.

- Explore the effects of messages received in childhood.

- Gain insight that will guide behavioral change.

- Focus thinking on behavioral goals for change.

- Uncover resources they possess that can help to cope with problems and difficulties.

- Identify personal characteristics without judgment.

- Develop full awareness of personal strengths and weaknesses.

Because the assessments are presented in a straightforward and easy-to-use format, individuals can self-administer, score, and interpret each assessment independently.

Introduction for the Participant

Relationships are an important aspect of everyone's lives, but with today's fast-paced electronic society, maintaining healthy, personal and intimate relationships are becoming more difficult. Like most successful things in life, relationships need care and work. For most of us, learning how to develop and nurture our relationships was not included in our education. This book, *The Personal and Intimate Relationship Skills Workbook* is intended to teach you the skills to build and maintain effective and healthy, personal and intimate relationships.

The Personal and Intimate Relationship Skills Workbook will help you grow personally and in your relationships. Because relationships can be a great source of both joy and pain, you will learn the skills required to get the most joy from your relationships. You will be encouraged throughout the workbook to complete assessments, journaling activities and exercises. Because involvement and action are as essential as theories, it is important that you take the time to complete all of the skill-building exercises.

The Personal and Intimate Relationship Skills Workbook, is designed to help you learn more about yourself, identify the effective and ineffective aspects of your relationships, and find better ways to use these newfound skills to develop and maintain happy, healthy relationships.

You will be asked to answer questions based on your current relationships or on ones from the past. This workbook is unique because several of the assessments have included space for you to complete the items based on *your* perspective, and then a space for you to answer the questions based on how you view *your partner's* perspective. If you are not currently in a relationship, you can complete the items based on a past relationship. The results will be most effective if you refer to the same relationship throughout the book, whether past or present.

The Personal and Intimate Relationship Skills Workbook

TABLE OF CONTENTS

TABLE OF CONTENTS *(continued)*

TABLE OF CONTENTS *(continued)*

TABLE OF CONTENTS *(continued)*

SECTION I:
Partner Communication Skills Scale

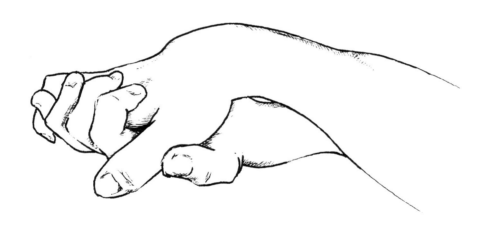

NAME _____   DATE _____

The relationship I will be referring to is with . . .

_____

Partner Communication Skills
Scale Directions

Communication is the exchanging of thoughts, opinions and information. It is the way you relate with your partner. Communication involves talking and listening to your partner, asserting yourself when you need to and arguing appropriately. Whether you are sharing personal experiences or talking about what each of you would like for dinner, you are using communication skills. Open, honest and direct communication is critical in any healthy relationship.

The Partner Communications Skills Scale can help you explore how effective you are when you interact with your partner. This assessment contains 50 statements. Read each of the statements and decide how much you agree. **In each of the choices listed, circle the number of your response to the left side of the line and then circle the number that you feel is correct for your partner on the right side of the line.**

In the following example, the circled **F** to the left of the line indicates that the statement is FALSE for the person completing the scale and the circled **T** to the right of the line indicates that the person completing the scale felt the statement was TRUE for their partner.

	You	Your Partner

When my partner and I are talking to each other we . . .

1. deliver clear messages to each other. . . . . T   (F)   (T)   F

This is not a test and there are no right or wrong answers. Do not spend too much time thinking about your answers. Your initial response will likely be the most true for you. Be sure to respond to every statement.

(Turn to the next page and begin)

Partner Communication Skills Scale

	You		Your Partner	

When my partner and I are talking to each other we . . .

	You		Your Partner	
1. deliver clear messages to each other. . . . . T	F		T	F
2. usually understand what the other is saying . . . . T	F		T	F
3. will clarify each other's position on issues to ensure understanding . . . . T	F		T	F
4. are straightforward in expressing our ideas . . . . T	F		T	F
5. say things so the other does not have to be a mind reader . . . . T	F		T	F
6. check to make sure the other hears and understands what we say. . . . . T	F		T	F
7. use "I" statements to take responsibility for what we are saying T	F		T	F
8. will ask for feedback about the messages we communicate . . . . T	F		T	F
9. make sure the other understands our nonverbal cues. . . . . T	F		T	F
10. talk for ourselves, not "everybody" . . . . T	F		T	F

DIRECT MESSAGES TOTAL T = _____   _____

	You		Your Partner	

When my partner and I disagree about something we . . .

	You		Your Partner	
11. blame the other . . . . T	F		T	F
12. make threats like "I will leave you..." . . . . T	F		T	F
13. use judgmental terms like "childish" and "helpless". . . . . T	F		T	F
14. call our partner names using global labels like "crazy" and "lazy" T	F		T	F
15. bring up old history. . . . . T	F		T	F
16. often make the other feel bad . . . . T	F		T	F
17. use sarcastic and demeaning words, comments and gestures . . T	F		T	F
18. often raise our voices, even though we may not be aware of it T	F		T	F
19. send negative messages . . . . T	F		T	F
20. become very defensive . . . . T	F		T	F

DISAGREEING AND ARGUING TOTAL F = _____   _____

(Continued on the next page)

(Partner Communication Skills Scale *continued*)

	You		Your Partner	

When my partner and I ask too much of each other we . . .

	You		Your Partner	
21. think it is selfish to put personal needs before each other's needs	T	F	T	F
22. fear disagreeing with each other	T	F	T	F
23. have a hard time standing up for ourselves	T	F	T	F
24. wish we could be more assertive	T	F	T	F
25. have trouble asking each other for what we need	T	F	T	F
26. will not express opinions that are different from each other's	T	F	T	F
27. do not like to make each other angry, so we go along	T	F	T	F
28. rarely question the other	T	F	T	F
29. hesitate to tell each other how we feel	T	F	T	F
30. always try to accommodate each other	T	F	T	F

BEING ASSERTIVE TOTAL F = _____   _____

	You		Your Partner	

When my partner and I listen to each other we . . .

	You		Your Partner	
31. are good at reading the non-verbal cues the other provides	T	F	T	F
32. usually hear each other's words	T	F	T	F
33. do not interrupt each other	T	F	T	F
34. ask for clarification if we do not understand something said	T	F	T	F
35. note each other's emotional tone	T	F	T	F
36. are careful to display positive body language	T	F	T	F
37. allow each other enough time to express a viewpoint	T	F	T	F
38. try not to get defensive	T	F	T	F
39. try to remain optimistic	T	F	T	F
40. try to see the situation from each other's point of view	T	F	T	F

ACTIVELY LISTENING TOTAL T = _____   _____

(Continued on the next page)

(Partner Communication Skills Scale *continued*)

	You		Your Partner	
When my partner and I argue we . . .				
41. respond to anger with anger	T	F	T	F
42. retaliate by insults with insults	T	F	T	F
43. tease each other too much	T	F	T	F
44. complain about the other a lot.	T	F	T	F
45. state our complaints in a heated way	T	F	T	F
46. frequently bring up each other's past failures	T	F	T	F
47. make harsh remarks	T	F	T	F
48. make physical attacks	T	F	T	F
49. lose control once we get started	T	F	T	F
50. criticize each other harshly	T	F	T	F

CRITICIZING AND FIGHTING TOTAL F = _____   _____

(Go to the Scoring Directions on the next page)

Partner Communication Skills Scale Scoring Directions

The Partner Communications Skills Scale is designed to measure how well you are able to communicate with your partner. Five important aspects of communicating effectively include sending direct messages, having controlled arguments, being assertive when you need to be, listening actively to what your partner says, and criticizing and arguing fairly. These make up the five scales on the assessment.

Scoring the assessment is a very easy process. Look at the questions you just answered.

- For Items **1-10**, count the number of **T** answers you circled for yourself and for your partner. Put those scores on the lines underneath each column **(DIRECT MESSAGES)**

- For Items **11-20**, count the number of **F** answers you circled for yourself and for your partner. Put those scores on the lines underneath each column **(DISAGREEING AND ARGUING)**

- For Items **21-30**, count the number of **F** answers you circled for yourself and for your partner. Put those scores on the lines underneath each column **(BEING ASSERTIVE)**

- For Items **31-40**, count the number of **T** answers you circled for yourself and for your partner. Put those scores on the lines underneath each column **(ACTIVELY LISTENING)**

- For Items **41-50**, count the number of **F** answers you circled for yourself and for your partner. Put those scores on the lines underneath each column **(CRITICIZING AND FIGHTING)**

Now, transfer your totals to the spaces below:

Direct Messages	You = _____	Your Partner = _____
Disagreeing and Arguing	You = _____	Your Partner = _____
Being Assertive	You = _____	Your Partner = _____
Actively Listening	You = _____	Your Partner = _____
Criticizing and Fighting	You = _____	Your Partner = _____

What patterns do you notice?

_____

_____

How do these results raise your awareness of your relationship with your partner?

_____

_____

What are the most critical areas for you and your partner to work on?

_____

_____

Partner Communication Skills Scale
Profile Interpretation

Communication is the essence of social interaction and often determines how successful you are in your relationship with your partner. This assessment will help you explore how effective you are in five critical components of effective communication. See the profile interpretation materials below.

TOTAL SCALES SCORES	RESULT	INDICATIONS
Scores from 16 to 20	High	You use effective communication skills a great deal of the time. Continue to use these effective communication skills when interacting with your partner. You will enjoy completing the exercises in this chapter.
Scores from 10 to 15	Moderate	Most of the time, you use effective communication skills. Continue to use the communication skills you are already using when interacting with your partner, and complete the exercises contained in this chapter for even more effective communication.
Scores from 5 to 9	Low	You are often not using effective communication skills with your partner. Complete the exercises contained in this chapter to assist you in discovering more effective communication skills with your partner.

Regardless of your score on the assessment, the following exercises have been designed to help you increase your communication skills.

Messages

To communicate effectively, it is necessary that you send clear messages to your partner and that your messages are completely understood. Miscommunication is probably the cause of many of your arguments and fights. By learning some specific skills you can ensure that the arguments between you and your partner are kept to a minimum. To be more effective in verbal communication with your partner, consider these guidelines to make certain your message is heard and accepted by your partner.

- **When you communicate verbally with your partner, take responsibility for your messages.** Use words like I, me and my, to communicate your message. In this way you "own" the messages you send to your partner. When you use words like "they" or "some people," you put the responsibility of what you are communicating onto someone else. Take responsibility for your own words. Using "you" often sounds threatening, aggressive and blaming, whereas creating I-messages conveys comments in the least threatening and overbearing manner.

- **Maintain eye contact and speak directly to your partner.** When asking questions, avoid dead-ended questions that require a yes-no answer ("Did you cook dinner like I asked?"). Instead, rely on open-ended questions that allow your partner the opportunity to express what happened ("What did you do this afternoon?").

- **Express your feelings.** Examples of how to express your feelings include such statements as "I feel angry when you get home so late from work without calling me" or "I get frustrated when you refuse to pay attention to the children." In the boxes on the left-hand side of the table, list the situations that frustrate you most about your partner. In the right-hand column, express your feelings to that person, using the guidelines you just read about.

Now You Try

Situations That Frustrate Me	What I Would Like to Say to My Partner
Ex: My partner doesn't call me when coming home late.	Ex: I would appreciate a phone call if you will be late. Then I will not feel concerned or will not worry.

Disagreeing and Arguing

Disagreements are not always unhealthy in a relationship, but they can lead to arguments. What do you and your partner tend to disagree about most? Disagreements often arise from not truly understanding what is going on in your partner's mind. When you find yourself beginning an argument with your partner, try to understand what is really happening and what you and your partner are really arguing about. In the left-hand column of the table that follows, list the things that trigger most of the arguments between you and your partner. Then, in the right-hand column, try to get to the bottom of the issues and see what is really triggering most of your fights.

Triggers for arguments	What we are really arguing about
Ex: Going to my partner's parents' home for dinner AGAIN!	Ex: We don't spend as much time with my parents!

Assertiveness

Assertiveness is the ability to ask for what you need and want in your relationship. Assertive people are able to express their feelings, thoughts, desires, needs and wants calmly and directly to their partner in an honest manner. This takes practice.

Why do you have a difficult time asking your partner what you need and want?

_____

_____

_____

What happens when you do?

_____

_____

_____

My Complaints or Dissatisfactions

In the table below, list some of your concerns and ways your partner can satisfy them.

Complaints or Dissatisfactions about my Partner	How My Partner Can Make me Happier
Ex: My partner does not show love, pride or affection when we are anywhere but home. I don't feel loved or attractive when we're in public.	Ex: My partner can put an arm around me, touch me, look at me with pride and love, tell people of my accomplishments, etc.

What I Want from My Partner

To assert yourself, you must know what you want from your partner and from your relationship with your partner. By establishing what it is that you really want, you will be able to ask for what you want and need without being afraid of angering your partner. You will be able to make decisions for yourself about what types of things you will need to be assertive. In the boxes on the right, list what you want from your partner in each of the categories in the left column.

Family	*Ex: I want my partner not to be upset when I want to spend an evening with my sister.*
Friends	
Finances	
Work	
Spirituality/Religion	
Children	
Household Duties	
Intimacy/Sex	
Social Activities	
Community	
Pets	
Other	
Other	

Non-Assertive Partner Situations

Identify those situations in which you need to be more assertive with your partner. By becoming more aware of those situations in which you are not assertive, you can practice your assertiveness training skills. For each of the situations listed below, describe how you show a lack of assertiveness.

Situations in which you might lack assertiveness	If you do lack assertiveness in this area, why aren't you assertive?
Saying "No" to your partner	*Ex: It hurts my partner's feelings and I don't want to do that.*
Asking my partner for favors	
Disagreeing with your partner's opinions	
Taking charge of a situation	
Social situations with your partner	
Asking for something you want from your partner	
Stating your opinion if it is different from your partner's opinion	
Asking for help from your partner	
Sexual situations with your partner	
Asking for time by yourself	

Listening

Active listening skills are often overlooked in a relationship, but can be one of the most critical aspects of communication and understanding between you and your partner. Active listening involves an awareness of what your partner is saying to you or asking you to do. Your active listening skills ensure that you understand the true meaning of the request or statement.

Blocks to Listening

Inadequate listening – It is easy to get distracted from what your partner is saying. This includes such things as being too involved with your own thoughts or preoccupied with your own needs. Perhaps you are thinking about your own problems or are too eager to help the other person. Possibly the social and cultural differences between you and your partner are too great.

Judging – Listening with the intent of judging your partner can hinder your ability to really hear what is being said. You may find that you are judging what your partner is saying as good or bad, right or wrong. You may not be listening with empathy. It is important to set your judgments aside about your partner until you can develop a better understanding of what your partner is saying and hear your partner's point of view on the issue.

Daydreaming – Everyone's attention wanders from time to time. If you find yourself having a difficult time listening to your partner, it is probably a sign that you are avoiding certain topics of conversation or that you are bored with what your partner is talking about.

Rehearsing – Any time you ask yourself the question "How should I respond to what my partner is saying?" or start rehearsing the way you will answer, you distract yourself from what the other person is saying. As you improve your active listening skills, the words just come naturally. It is best to listen intently to your partner and to focus on the themes and core messages related to their words, and allow your intuition to provide you with a response.

Filtering – Listening to certain parts of the conversation, but not all, can cause trouble. You'll only get a portion of the facts and you will base responses or actions on just part of what you needed to hear.

Distractions – Your attention is sidetracked by something internal to you (hunger, headache, worry) or external to you (traffic, whispering, other people). Concentrating on the conversation and staying in the present will help.

Learning to Listen

Listening can be a difficult skill to master because it requires you to hear with your eyes, body and heart, as well as with your ears.

Effective Listening Skills
Focus on what your partner is saying paying no attention to internal or external happenings.
Listen to the words, tone of voice, notice the body language, feel the sincerity.
Clarify misunderstood points ("What did you mean when you said_____").
Ask questions for more information or clarification ("What do you need from me right now?").

Non-Effective Listening Skills
Focus on your feelings about what your partner is saying.
Listen to the words only and do not pay attention to body language and sincerity.
Feel defensive and rehearse in your mind how to respond.
Judge, label and make assumptions about what is being said.

What do you notice about your listening habits when communicating with your partner?

_____

_____

_____

What do you notice about your partner's listening habits when communicating with you?

_____

_____

_____

How can you be a better listener?

_____

_____

_____

In which situations can you be a better listener for your partner?

_____

_____

_____

Anger

People in healthy relationships still argue, but when they do, it is not a vicious fight – it's a discussion because partners in a close and personal relationship are able to express their opinions and needs without hurting each other physically, verbally or psychologically. Partners are able to resolve their differences and solve problems by compromising and working together to find win-win solutions.

Ways to Avoid Arguments

Leave the situation until your angry feelings have passed. Take a walk, browse in a bookstore, visit a neighbor or go to the gym until you ready to discuss the situation more rationally. What types of things could you do the next time you feel an argument escalating?

_____

_____

_____

Use empathy to better understand. Empathy is the ability to put yourself in your partner's shoes and experience what he or she is experiencing. Think about some situations about which you and your partner argue. List those situations in the left column of the table below. Then in the right column, list some of your insights about the situation, putting yourself in your partner's situation.

Things we argue about	Insights about why we argue
Ex: I often spend money on something for myself and my partner gets upset.	Ex: My partner works very hard and doesn't understand buying anything that we don't need. If I had discussed it before, it might have been okay.

Avoid Jumping to Conclusions

False assumptions happen when you or your partner jump to conclusions about each other's thoughts, feelings or actions.

Ways I Jump to Conclusions About My Partner
Ex: When my partner is late coming home, I assume he's cheating on me.

Ways My Partner Jumps to Conclusions About Me
Ex: When I say we don't have enough money my partner assumes I want her to work more hours.

Communication Skills

Which communication skills do you need most to improve? How will you do that?

_____

_____

_____

_____

_____

_____

How do you feel these communication skills will directly impact your relationship with your partner?

_____

_____

_____

_____

_____

_____

_____

Which communication skills could your partner develop?

_____

_____

_____

_____

_____

_____

_____

Communication Skills Quotations

☐ *Someone to tell it to is one of the fundamental needs of human beings.*

—Miles Franklin

☐ *I felt it shelter to speak with you.*

—Emily Dickinson

Check one of the above quotations and journal your thoughts on how it applies to you.

_____

_____

_____

_____

_____

_____

_____

_____

_____

_____

_____

_____

_____

_____

_____

_____

Communication Pitfalls

- Feeling that your partner is at fault, you are the victim and there is nothing you can do about it

- Feeling defensive if your partner has an opinion that is different from yours

- Maintaining a pessimistic outlook about your partner

- Rejecting and devaluing your partner

- Expecting a change in personality in your partner

- Exchanging unclear and mixed messages with your partner

- Digging up the past with your partner

- Arguing for the sake of arguing

Facts About Communication in a Healthy, Personal and Close Relationship

- Good communication means being open, honest and direct

- Effective communication is essential

- Good communication involves sending direct, clear verbal messages, listening actively, asserting yourself when you need to and overcoming arguments with calm and patience

- Communication occurs not only with words, but also through body language, gestures, and tone, volume and pitch of voice

- Rewards of a healthy relationship are:

    - Mutual understanding

    - Less chance of conflict

    - Cooperation

    - Meeting needs while your needs are being met

    - Relief from negative emotions

    - Enhanced closeness

SECTION II:
Personality Scale

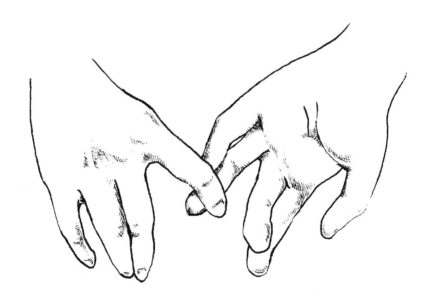

NAME _____ DATE _____

The relationship I will be referring to is with . . .

_____

Personality Scale Directions

Personalities are consistent styles of behavior and emotional reactions that are present from infancy onward. They develop as a result of a combination of heredity and early environmental experiences. People have different types of personalities. The better you and your partner understand your own and each other's personality characteristics, the more satisfying and compatible your relationship will be.

The Partner Personality Scale contains a series of words that describe various personality traits that you may or may not display. Read each of the words listed and decide whether or not the word describes you. If it does describe you, circle the word in the column. If it does not describe you, do not circle the word, simply move to the next word.

This is not a test and there are no right or wrong answers. Do not spend too much time thinking about your answers but be sure to read and respond to every word listed, either by circling it or not. Your initial response will likely be the most true for you.

I consider MYSELF to be *(circle all that apply):*

Conforming	Humble	(Athletic)
Frank	Handy	Persistent
(Genuine)	Sensible	(Practical)
Hard-headed	(Natural)	Shy
Honest	Mechanical	(Outdoorsy)
(Stable)	Self-reliant	Physical

R TOTAL = _____

In the above example, the test taker is genuine, stable, natural, athletic, practical and outdoorsy. Remember that you do not need to circle any of the words if you feel that none of them apply or you may circle as many as do apply to you.

(Turn to the next page and begin)

Personality Scale

I consider MYSELF to be (circle all that apply):

Conforming	Humble	Athletic
Frank	Handy	Persistent
Genuine	Sensible	Practical
Hard-headed	Natural	Shy
Honest	Mechanical	Outdoorsy
Stable	Self-reliant	Physical

R TOTAL = _____

I consider MYSELF to be (circle all that apply):

Analytical	Resourceful	Modest
Cautious	Intellectual	Pessimistic
Complex	Introverted	Precise
Critical	Methodical	Rational
Curious	Logical	Reserved
Scientific	Scholarly	Self-controlled

I TOTAL = _____

I consider MYSELF to be (circle all that apply):

Complicated	Imaginative	Creative
Individualistic	Innovative	Intuitive
Emotional	Impulsive	Nonconforming
Expressive	Independent	Open
Idealistic	Artsy	Original
Uncontrolled	Daydreamy	Unstructured

A TOTAL = _____

(Continued on the next page)

(**MY Personality Scale** *continued*)

I consider MYSELF to be *(circle all that apply):*

Convincing	Light-hearted	Sociable
Cooperative	Kind	Friendly
Emotional	Patient	Tactful
Generous	Responsible	Understanding
Helpful	Caring	Warm
Humanistic	People-oriented	Cheerful

S TOTAL = _____

I consider MYSELF to be *(circle all that apply):*

Inquisitive	Domineering	Optimistic
Adventurous	Energetic	Assertive
Bold	Extroverted	Popular
Ambitious	Impulsive	Self-confident
Attention-getting	Persuasive	Sociable
Aggressive	Charismatic	Goal-driven

E TOTAL = _____

I consider MYSELF to be *(circle all that apply):*

Conforming	Inhibited	Persistent
Conscientious	Obedient	Practical
Careful	Orderly	Thrifty
Efficient	Unimaginative	Reserved
Structured	Precise	Detail-oriented
Scheduled	Dependable	Self-controlled

C TOTAL = _____

(Go to the Scoring Directions on the next page)

My Personality Scale Scoring

Count the total number of items you circled for each section. Put that number on the line marked TOTAL at the bottom of each of section and then transfer your totals in the spaces below.

R _____ = Realistic

I _____ = Investigative

A _____ = Artistic

S _____ = Social

E _____ = Enterprising

C _____ = Conventional

Profile Interpretation

INDIVIDUAL SCALE SCORES	RESULT	INDICATIONS
Scores from 0 to 5	Low	You do not possess many of the characteristics of this personality type.
Scores from 6 to 12	Moderate	You possess some of the characteristics of this personality type.
Scores from 13 to 18	High	You possess many of the characteristics of this personality type.

Generally the higher your score, the more characteristics you share with others of that personality type. Identify the scale on which you scored the highest. This is your primary personality type.

Research indicates that people tend to commit to relationships with people who have similar attitudes, values and interests. However, as relationships grow and develop, personality differences often influence marital happiness and longevity. One of the reasons for this is that being in a long-term relationship requires regular interaction between you and your partner, and cooperation and compatibility in dealing with the problems of daily living. These tasks are required in a partnership to solve personal issues inherent in any relationship. Similar personality types for you and your partner can facilitate cooperation, but personality differences may result in more conflict in daily living. However, you have probably heard the old saying "opposites attract" and may know couples who have lived happily even though they had different personality types. If you and your partner do have different personality types, it is important to acknowledge the characteristics of your own type while being open-minded enough to appreciate the personality characteristics of your partner.

Vocational psychologist John Holland theorizes that all people are made up of some combination of the above six types of personalities. Each of the following descriptions represents "pure" types. You will probably see some parts of each description fitting you in different roles you play. Keep this in mind as you read the description of each type. Read about your personality type(s) as well as all of the other types in the descriptions that follow. Complete the questions at the bottom of the descriptions.

Scale Description for Realistic Personality

People scoring high on the Realistic Scale enjoy the practical aspects of a relationship. They tend to be reliable and dependable partners in a relationship. They take their obligations seriously and honor their commitments. They like the predictability of being in a relationship. They focus on the day-to-day business of living and enjoy doing practical things like mowing the lawn, cooking, fixing the car, cleaning and paying bills. They enjoy working on outside activities or activities with machines rather than with people. They tend not to be very interested in social activities and would much rather be outdoors.

Realistic personalities are cultivators; they have an urge to make things grow and prosper. They are primarily interested in practical, earthy matters, granting them the ability to develop the things they feel are most worthy, like a building, business or relationship. They tend to have a no-nonsense approach to life.

Realistic personalities are not always interested in prestige or financial rewards that come with accomplishments — they simply enjoy getting things done. They are also not interested in generating ideas, being innovative or in trying to understand complex formulas. Instead they enjoy things that are easy to experience and that they can feel, taste, hear and smell.

Realistic personalities seek stability and security in their relationships. They are reliable, stubborn, down-to-earth, autonomous and true to their word.

In what ways does this description fit you?

_____

_____

_____

_____

_____

In what ways does this description not fit you?

_____

_____

_____

_____

_____

Scale Description for Investigative Personality

People scoring high on the Investigative Scale enjoy being challenged intellectually when in a relationship. They are bright and curious, and tend to be lifelong students. They are very inquisitive and are driven by the desire to research and learn new things and search for answers to life's mysteries. They are often perceived as being scholarly, analytic, critical, curious, introspective and methodical.

Investigative personalities are often absorbed in the world of ideas and concepts and lose sight of the importance of a good relationship with their partner. They enjoy debating their ideas with others, but they also spend a lot of time observing others from a detached point of view. This can cause communication problems in some relationships. They usually enjoy leisure activities like reading books and going to concerts, theatre productions, museums and lectures.

Investigative personalities are most comfortable thinking rather than feeling or acting. They usually evaluate, process and synthesize information. They do not get bogged down in details but always keep the big picture in mind. For the investigative personality, understanding life is just as much fun as living it.

Investigative personalities tend to be quiet and introspective, and spend a lot of time alone. They usually become focused on becoming an expert in one area of interest and will devote a lifetime to this interest if it helps to develop their identity. Because of this intensity, they often prefer partners who are independent and self-reliant.

In what ways does this description fit you?

_____

_____

_____

_____

_____

In what ways does this description not fit you?

_____

_____

_____

_____

_____

Scale Description for Artistic Personality

People scoring high on the Artistic Scale tend to see life and relationships from a holistic perspective that allows them to always be looking at the big picture. They avoid highly structured situations and involve themselves totally in their creative endeavors.

Artistic personalities are able to create vivid pictures in their mind. This allows them to create novel applications to existing services, products and projects. They are continually looking for new interests and often have difficulty staying with tasks until their completion, often making their efforts long on vision and a little short on action.

Artistic personalities strive to make the world a better and different place through their creative endeavors. Their creativity is expressed through a variety of activities including music, dance, writing, entertainment, art in any form, etc. Nearly everything they do is connected with being able to express their uniqueness and individuality. They have a very highly developed aesthetic sense and are often asked to bring new perspectives to traditional problems.

Creative personalities tend to be shy and introverted and thus are not usually comfortable in the standard business world. They find typical eight-to-five jobs too restrictive, and they do not like taking orders from other people, even a supervisor. They therefore tend to work alone, toiling tirelessly to see their creations come to fruition.

In what ways does this description fit you?

_____

_____

_____

_____

_____

In what ways does this description not fit you?

_____

_____

_____

_____

_____

Scale Description for Social Personality

People who score high on the Social Scale are able to be aware of their partner's deep emotions and are sensitive to their needs. They like to work cooperatively with their partner when a problem arises. They also have a strong concern for the welfare of others. Their mission in life tends to be selfless and they give more than they take. They are compassionate and nurturing.

Social personalities are interested in helping and working in their community, whether through spiritual service, counseling, teaching or medicine. They prefer to deal with people rather than with ideas or things. They value the spiritual and emotional rewards they receive from their partner. They are willing and eager to work on themselves and work on improving their relationships.

Social personalities often invest a great deal of effort, emotion and enthusiasm in their relationships, but sometimes more than is needed. While their life and their relationships tend to be practical in nature, they are often driven by a philosophical stance that focuses on long-range problems and concerns. Other people often view them as being idealistic.

Social personalities are determined to stick to their principles and they strive to find a partner who has similar values. They are very thoughtful and emotional, but are equally capable of taking quick and decisive action for the benefit of others. They value depth and authenticity in their relationships.

In what ways does this description fit you?

_____

_____

_____

_____

_____

In what ways does this description not fit you?

_____

_____

_____

_____

_____

Scale Description for Enterprising Personality

People who score high on the Enterprising Scale like to take the lead and be assertive in their relationships. They tend to value the rewards that come with power, status and a higher-than-average income. They strive to be the best at what they do and to be the first to do it. They are confident and determined and have natural leadership abilities; in many cases they just prefer to do things themselves. They are also highly persuasive and charismatic in a relationship.

Enterprising personalities prefer to be in charge. They make decisions quickly and decisively whether others like it or not. They understand power and the impact that it can have on their life and the life of their partner. They also have a talent for bringing out the power of other people. They tend to understand and appreciate the power of money, and they strive to attain it, control it and put it to good use.

Enterprising personalities are usually eager to initiate new projects and take on new challenges. Their confidence and determination makes "all things possible," and allows them to succeed in the fast-paced world of business. They are always looking for the next project to work on and tend to focus on positive opportunities rather than negative consequences. Perhaps more than any other personality, they are the most driven to pursue one standard definition of success; climbing the ladder, or building one of their own, to achieve wealth, prestige and happiness.

In what ways does this description fit you?

_____

_____

_____

_____

_____

In what ways does this description not fit you?

_____

_____

_____

_____

Scale Description for Conventional Personality

People who score high on the Conventional Scale tend to be neat, organized and always under control in their relationships. They are able to concentrate on the task at hand and are excellent with details. They are orderly to the point of sometimes being inflexible and they prefer to follow strict guidelines.

Conventional personalities often prefer activities that involve data and information rather than people or ideas. They have extraordinary detail orientation and are often counted on for their dependability and reliability in a relationship. They are practical and hardworking. They enjoy solving problems provided there is a set procedure to follow. They make excellent day-to-day managers of life, though they prefer to run and organize their relationships from behind the scenes.

Conventional personalities truly value success in a relationship and will do everything in their power to ensure that success. They are conscientious, stable, thorough and conservative, enjoying life when everything runs according to plan.

In what ways does this description fit you?

_____

_____

_____

_____

_____

In what ways does this description not fit you?

_____

_____

_____

_____

_____

_____

How I View My Partner's Personality

Now, retake the assessment, but this time circle descriptors based on how you view your partner's personality.

I consider my PARTNER to be *(circle all that apply)*:

Conforming	Humble	Athletic
Frank	Handy	Persistent
Genuine	Sensible	Practical
Hard-headed	Natural	Shy
Honest	Mechanical	Outdoorsy
Stable	Self-reliant	Physical

R TOTAL = _____

I consider my PARTNER to be *(circle all that apply)*:

Analytical	Resourceful	Modest
Cautious	Intellectual	Pessimistic
Complex	Introverted	Precise
Critical	Methodical	Rational
Curious	Logical	Reserved
Scientific	Scholarly	Self-controlled

I TOTAL = _____

I consider my PARTNER to be *(circle all that apply)*:

Complicated	Imaginative	Creative
Individualistic	Innovative	Intuitive
Emotional	Impulsive	Nonconforming
Expressive	Independent	Open
Idealistic	Artsy	Original
Uncontrolled	Daydreamy	Unstructured

A TOTAL = _____

(Continued on the next page)

(How I View My Partner's Personality Scale *continued*)

I consider my PARTNER to be *(circle all that apply)*:

Convincing	Light-hearted	Sociable
Cooperative	Kind	Friendly
Emotional	Patient	Tactful
Generous	Responsible	Understanding
Helpful	Caring	Warm
Humanistic	People-oriented	Cheerful

S TOTAL = _____

I consider my PARTNER to be *(circle all that apply)*:

Inquisitive	Domineering	Optimistic
Adventurous	Energetic	Assertive
Bold	Extroverted	Popular
Ambitious	Impulsive	Self-confident
Attention-getting	Persuasive	Sociable
Aggressive	Charismatic	Goal-driven

E TOTAL = _____

I consider my PARTNER to be *(circle all that apply)*:

Conforming	Inhibited	Persistent
Conscientious	Obedient	Practical
Careful	Orderly	Thrifty
Efficient	Unimaginative	Reserved
Structured	Precise	Detail-oriented
Scheduled	Dependable	Self-controlled

C TOTAL = _____

(Go to the Scoring Directions on the next page)

How I View My Partner's Personality Scale Scoring

Count the total number of items you circled for each section. Put that number on the line marked TOTAL at the bottom of each of section and then transfer your totals in the spaces below.

R _____ = Realistic

I _____ = Investigative

A _____ = Artistic

S _____ = Social

E _____ = Enterprising

C _____ = Conventional

Profile Interpretation

INDIVIDUAL SCALE SCORES	RESULT	INDICATIONS
Scores from 0 to 5	Low	In your perception, your partner does not possess many of the characteristics of this personality type.
Scores from 6 to 12	Moderate	In your perception, your partner possesses some of the characteristics of this personality type.
Scores from 13 to 18	High	In your perception, your partner possesses many of the characteristics of this personality type.

Comparing Personalities

You can now compare your personality with that of your partner. List your scores and your partner's scores for the six scales. Compare and contrast the results. Remember that similar personality types can facilitate cooperation and different personality types can work if both people are open-minded with the ability to compromise and adjust when needed. Knowing the differences in your personalities and the way you communicate is an important factor to your relationship being successful, exciting and stimulating.

Myself	Personality Scales	My Partner
	R (Realistic)	
	I (Investigative)	
	A (Artistic)	
	S (Social)	
	E (Enterprising)	
	C (Conventional)	

How were the scores for you and your partner on the assessments similar?

_____

_____

How were the scores for you and your partner on the assessments different?

_____

_____

How do the similarities enhance your relationship? How do they detract from the relationship?

_____

_____

How do the differences enhance your relationship? How do they detract from the relationship?

_____

_____

Are you and your partner good communicators with the ability to compromise and adjust?

_____

_____

Personality Changes

Your personality type has been influenced by both your early life experiences as well as your heredity. Therefore, your personality type has been maturing and developing since you were a child. By the time you reached your teen years, your personality type began to crystallize and become a part of who you are. It is very unlikely that your personality type has changed much and it rarely changes as you move through adulthood.

How has your personality changed over the years?

_____

_____

_____

How has your personality remained the same?

_____

_____

_____

What aspects of your personality would you like to change to be more compatible with your partner?

_____

_____

_____

What have you learned about your partner's personality?

_____

_____

_____

How will this help your relationship?

_____

_____

_____

Agreeing – Disagreeing

Based on your partner's and your personalities, what do you and your partner agree about most?

_____

_____

_____

_____

_____

_____

_____

_____

_____

Based on your partner's and your personalities, what do you and your partner disagree about most?

_____

_____

_____

_____

_____

_____

_____

_____

_____

_____

Partner Personality Quotations

☐ *People change and forget to tell each other.*

—Lillian Hellman

☐ *Are we not like two volumes of one book?*

—Marceline Desborders-Valmore

Check one of the above quotations and journal your thoughts on how it applies, or does not apply, to you.

_____

_____

_____

_____

_____

_____

_____

_____

_____

_____

_____

_____

_____

_____

_____

_____

_____

_____

Aspects of Personality Types

- You probably cannot change your basic personality type, but you can change behaviors associated with your basic type.

- All types have unique sets of strengths and weaknesses.

- No personality type is better than other personality types.

- All of the information you read about your type may not apply to you all of the time.

- People with similar personality types tend to be motivated in the same ways, view the world in a similar manner, and engage in similar occupations and leisure activities.

- Factors such as where you were born and raised, your family's socio-economic status, and the cultural values you inherit can influence the intensity of your personality type.

- Partners do not necessarily need to have similar personality types to have a great relationship.

Personality and Relationships

Your personality affects your relationships in a variety of ways including . . .

- How you approach decision making

- Why you are drawn to certain occupations

- Why you prefer certain hobbies and leisure-time activities

- How you interact with other people

- How you experience time

- How you recognize and value diversity in others

- How you solve problems and resolve conflicts

- How seriously you take your commitments

- Whether you look at 'the big picture'

- How you feel about community

SECTION III:
Relationship Needs Scale

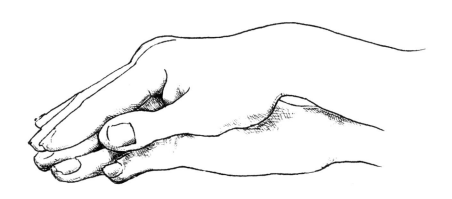

NAME _____   DATE _____

The relationship I will be referring to is with . . .

_____

Relationship Needs Scale Directions

All people have a complexity of needs: emotional, spiritual, social, sharing, sense-of-security and financial. Needs are elements and conditions in your life that you feel must be present in order for you to be happy. People need different types of things and that can be problematic in some relationships, especially if these needs haven't been discussed ahead of time. The Relationship Needs Scale can help you identify and explore your dominant needs, as well as the needs of your partner, and then help you to determine your compatibility.

This assessment contains 49 statements. Use the choices listed below to respond to each statement both for you and your partner. If you are not currently in a relationship, you can complete the items based on someone from your past, or complete the items for you only. Read each of the statements and circle the number to the right of the first column, *Response About You*, that best describes how much you value each statement. Then, if applicable, circle the number in the second column, *Response About Your Partner*, which best describes how you perceive your partner would value the same statement.

Circle **4** if the statement is **Very Important**   Circle **2** if the statement is **Somewhat Important**
Circle **3** if the statement is **Important**   Circle **1** if the statement is **Not Important**

	Response About You	Response About Your Partner
EMOTIONAL NEEDS		
The need to feel like I am loved	(4) 3 2 1	4 3 2 (1)

This is not a test and there are no right or wrong answers. Do not spend too much time thinking about your answers. Your initial response will likely be the most true for you. Be sure to respond to every statement.

(Turn to the next page and begin)

Relationship Needs Scale

Circle **4** if the statement is **Very Important**   Circle **2** if the statement is **Somewhat Important**
Circle **3** if the statement is **Important**   Circle **1** if the statement is **Not Important**

	Response About You				Response About Your Partner			
EMOTIONAL NEEDS								
The need to feel I am loved	4	3	2	1	4	3	2	1
The need to feel that I am a priority in my partner's life	4	3	2	1	4	3	2	1
The need to feel respected by my partner	4	3	2	1	4	3	2	1
The need to feel accepted and appreciated for who I am	4	3	2	1	4	3	2	1
The need to feel like a close friend of my partner	4	3	2	1	4	3	2	1
The need to feel desired by my partner	4	3	2	1	4	3	2	1
The need to feel trusted as a partner	4	3	2	1	4	3	2	1

EMOTIONAL NEEDS TOTAL = _____   TOTAL = _____

	Response About You				Response About Your Partner			
PHYSICAL NEEDS								
The need to be kissed affectionately	4	3	2	1	4	3	2	1
The need to be physically welcomed by my partner	4	3	2	1	4	3	2	1
The need for satisfying sexual activity	4	3	2	1	4	3	2	1
The need to be touched and held	4	3	2	1	4	3	2	1
The need to feel loved expressed through nonverbal behaviors	4	3	2	1	4	3	2	1
The need to feel like a welcomed part of a couple	4	3	2	1	4	3	2	1
The need to feel comfortable in the personal space of my partner	4	3	2	1	4	3	2	1

PHYSICAL NEEDS TOTAL = _____   TOTAL = _____

	Response About You				Response About Your Partner			
SPIRITUAL NEEDS								
The need to know my beliefs are valued	4	3	2	1	4	3	2	1
The need to share a spiritual life with my partner	4	3	2	1	4	3	2	1
The need to know that my goals are important in a relationship	4	3	2	1	4	3	2	1
The need to know my spiritual values are important	4	3	2	1	4	3	2	1
The need to know I am supported in order to be all I can be	4	3	2	1	4	3	2	1
The need to feel as if my partner wants me to achieve my goals	4	3	2	1	4	3	2	1
The need to know that my relationship has meaning	4	3	2	1	4	3	2	1

SPIRITUAL NEEDS TOTAL = _____   TOTAL = _____

(Continued on the next page)

(Relationship Needs Scale *continued*)

Circle **4** if the statement is **Very Important**   Circle **2** if the statement is **Somewhat Important**
Circle **3** if the statement is **Important**   Circle **1** if the statement is **Not Important**

	Response About You				Response About Your Partner			
SOCIAL NEEDS								
The need to be treated respectfully in social situations	4	3	2	1	4	3	2	1
The need to have fun together in social situations	4	3	2	1	4	3	2	1
The need to have common leisure interests	4	3	2	1	4	3	2	1
The need to show affection in public places	4	3	2	1	4	3	2	1
The need to have my partner include me in social activities	4	3	2	1	4	3	2	1
The need to be encouraged and supported in public	4	3	2	1	4	3	2	1
The need to be in contact when apart	4	3	2	1	4	3	2	1

SOCIAL NEEDS TOTAL = _____   TOTAL = _____

	Response About You				Response About Your Partner			
SHARING NEEDS								
The need to help out with the children	4	3	2	1	4	3	2	1
The need make enough money to support the household	4	3	2	1	4	3	2	1
The need to run errands when possible.	4	3	2	1	4	3	2	1
The need to interact with each other's families	4	3	2	1	4	3	2	1
The need to do household chores	4	3	2	1	4	3	2	1
The need to plan vacations and free-time activities	4	3	2	1	4	3	2	1
The need to cook and bake	4	3	2	1	4	3	2	1

SHARING NEEDS TOTAL = _____   TOTAL = _____

	Response About You				Response About Your Partner			
SENSE-OF-SECURITY NEEDS								
The need to know my partner will be available to me	4	3	2	1	4	3	2	1
The need to be supported in all my endeavors	4	3	2	1	4	3	2	1
The need to know my partner is loyal	4	3	2	1	4	3	2	1
The need to know my partner is committed to me	4	3	2	1	4	3	2	1
The need to know my partner is there for me in hard times	4	3	2	1	4	3	2	1
The need to know my partner will stick up for me	4	3	2	1	4	3	2	1
The need to know my partner will remain committed and not leave	4	3	2	1	4	3	2	1

SENSE-OF-SECURITY NEEDS TOTAL = _____   TOTAL = _____

(Continued on the next page)

(Relationship Needs Scale *continued*)

Circle **4** if the statement is **Very Important**   Circle **2** if the statement is **Somewhat Important**
Circle **3** if the statement is **Important**   Circle **1** if the statement is **Not Important**

FINANCIAL NEEDS	Response About You				Response About Your Partner			
The need to pay bills on time	4	3	2	1	4	3	2	1
The need to balance the checkbook	4	3	2	1	4	3	2	1
The need to budget and save money	4	3	2	1	4	3	2	1
The need to develop long-term financial goals	4	3	2	1	4	3	2	1
The need to spend money wisely	4	3	2	1	4	3	2	1
The need to share responsibility for managing money	4	3	2	1	4	3	2	1
The need to share money with people in need	4	3	2	1	4	3	2	1

FINANCIAL NEEDS TOTAL = _____   TOTAL = _____

(Go to the Scoring Directions on the next page)

© 2010 WHOLE PERSON ASSOCIATES, 210 WEST MICHIGAN ST., DULUTH MN 55802-1908 ▪ 800-247-6789

Relationship Needs
Scale Scoring Directions

It is important to understand your needs in a relationship as well as the needs of your partner. The Relationship Needs Scale is designed to measure the specific needs that you bring to a relationship and includes the needs of your partner. Remember that needs are different for all people and can be a source of great pleasure; absence or fulfillment of meeting one's needs often leads to a conflict in a relationship.

For each of the sections you completed, add the numbers you circled in the left-hand column for each section. Put that total on the line marked "Total" at the end of each section. If you also completed the scale for your partner, add the numbers you circled in the right-hand column for each section, and put that total on the line marked "Total" at the end of that section.

Then, transfer your totals (for both you and your partner) to the spaces below.

MY TOTALS		TOTALS FOR MY PARTNER	
Emotional Needs Total	= _____	Emotional Needs Total	= _____
Physical Needs Total	= _____	Physical Needs Total	= _____
Spiritual Needs Total	= _____	Spiritual Needs Total	= _____
Social Needs Total	= _____	Social Needs Total	= _____
Sharing Needs Total	= _____	Sharing Needs Total	= _____
Sense-of-Security Needs Total	= _____	Sense-of-Security Needs Total	= _____
Financial Needs Total	= _____	Financial Needs Total	= _____

Differences in Scores

There is great value in exploring your needs and the needs of your partner to gain a better understanding of how they impact your relationship. Identifying similarities and differences helps you to understand the dynamics of your relationship more clearly, accept differences in your partner more readily and enhance compatibility. Although you may find many differences in your needs profile and that of your partner, this is not necessarily negative and does not mean that you and your partner cannot have a happy relationship. When you are aware of your partner's strengths and complimentary gifts, you can more easily affirm rather than criticize, without being judgmental. Accepting each other's needs is an ongoing process within every relationship and is part of your growth together as a partnership. As you recognize and accept each other's needs patterns to be valid, you allow for compromise in your relationship, with both of you feeling satisfied.

Profile Interpretation

INDIVIDUAL SCALE SCORES	RESULT	INDICATIONS
Scores from 7 to 13	Low	These types of needs are not very important to you or to your partner. They would be considered less important needs.
Scores from 14 to 21	Moderate	These types of needs are somewhat important to you or to your partner. They would be considered secondary needs.
Scores from 12 to 28	High	These types of needs are very important to you or to your partner. They would be considered primary needs.

Scale Descriptions

EMOTIONAL NEEDS – People scoring high on this scale need to feel they are loved and respected by their partners. They want their partners to put them at the top of their priority list and feel trusted and desired by them. They expect their partners to love and accept them for who they are.

PHYSICAL NEEDS – People scoring high on this scale need to be touched and held, and feel comfortable with their partners. Physical aspects of a relationship are very important to them. They expect their partners to be affectionate when they are alone or in public.

SPIRITUAL NEEDS – People scoring high on this scale need a spiritual life and to share spiritual values with their partners. They need a relationship that provides them with meaning and one in which their beliefs are valued by their partners. They expect their partners to support them in achieving their goals and reaching their full potential.

SOCIAL NEEDS – People scoring high on this scale need to feel loved in social situations. They need their partners to stay in contact with them when they are apart and to engage in common leisure activities when they are together. They expect their partners to engage in many social activities with them.

SHARING NEEDS – People scoring high on this scale need to have partners who share with household and family responsibilities. They need to have partners who help around the house, share in raising and disciplining the children, and work to contribute to the financial success of the relationship.

SENSE-OF-SECURITY NEEDS – People scoring high on this scale need to feel safe and secure with their partner. They need to know that their partners are committed and loyal to them, and they expect support and availability from their partners.

FINANCIAL NEEDS – People scoring high on this scale need to have partners who share their thoughts about how to manage money in their relationship. They need to have partners who are responsible when it comes to financial matters. They expect their partners to spend, save and share money as they do.

The higher the total number for each section, the more important those needs are to you and your partner in achieving satisfaction in your relationship. No matter whether you scored *Low*, *Moderate* or *High*, the exercises and activities that follow are designed to help you explore how you and your partner meet (or fail to meet) each other's needs to maintain a healthy, satisfying relationship.

Emotional Needs

How do you and your partner show respect for each other? How do you not?

_____

_____

_____

In what ways do you and your partner show appreciation for one another? How do you not?

_____

_____

_____

How do you and your partner meet each other's emotional needs?

_____

_____

_____

How could you and your partner better meet each other's emotional needs?

_____

_____

_____

In what ways do you and your partner show trust for one another?

_____

_____

_____

In what ways do you and your partner not trust each other?

_____

_____

_____

Physical Needs

How do you and your partner express affection with each other, publicly and privately?

_____

_____

_____

_____

How do you meet your partner's physical needs?

_____

_____

_____

_____

How could you better meet your partner's physical needs?

_____

_____

_____

_____

How does your partner meet your physical needs?

_____

_____

_____

_____

How could your partner better meet your physical needs?

_____

_____

_____

_____

Spiritual Needs

How are your spiritual needs and those of your partner the same?

_____

_____

_____

How are your spiritual needs and those of your partner different?

_____

_____

_____

What types of spiritual activities do you like to do together?

_____

_____

_____

In what ways do spirituality and spiritual issues interfere with your relationship?

_____

_____

_____

What spiritual values do you share?

_____

_____

_____

What values do you each have that the other does not?

_____

_____

_____

Social Needs

What types of social situations do you and your partner share?

_____

_____

_____

What types of social occasions do you and your partner enjoy and have fun?

_____

_____

_____

What social happenings do you like that your partner does not?

_____

_____

_____

What social happenings does your partner like that you do not?

_____

_____

_____

How do you and your partner meet your social needs?

_____

_____

_____

How could you and your partner better meet your social needs?

_____

_____

_____

Sharing Needs

Describe how you and your partner share household responsibilities.

_____

_____

_____

In an ideal world, how could you and your partner be more responsible?

_____

_____

_____

How do you meet your partner's sharing needs?

_____

_____

_____

How could you better meet your partner's sharing needs?

_____

_____

_____

How does your partner meet your sharing needs?

_____

_____

_____

How could your partner better meet your sharing needs?

_____

_____

_____

Sense-of-Security Needs

How do you and your partner support each other?

_____

_____

_____

How can you and your partner support each other better?

_____

_____

_____

How do you and your partner help each other to feel secure in your relationship?

_____

_____

_____

What else can either one of you do to help the other feel more secure?

_____

_____

_____

How do you and your partner show loyalty and commitment to each other?

_____

_____

_____

What else can either one of you do to show loyalty and commitment to each other?

_____

_____

_____

Financial Needs

What types of financial goals do you and your partner share?

_____

_____

_____

What money issues do you disagree about most?

_____

_____

_____

How do you manage the daily money issues (paying bills, etc.) with your partner?

_____

_____

_____

How does that work for both of you?

_____

_____

_____

How are your spending habits the same? Different?

_____

_____

_____

How are your saving habits the same? Different?

_____

_____

_____

Dealing with Incompatibility

You and your partner can work to overcome any incompatibilities you may be experiencing in your relationship. Try the following exercise.

1) What is the most important issue in which you feel you and your partner are incompatible?

_____

_____

_____

2) How do you and your partner differ?

_____

_____

_____

3) What might be the reasons you differ? (how you were raised, your ethnic or cultural backgrounds, religious ideals, values, etc.)?

_____

_____

_____

4) How can you and your partner come up with a plan for being more compatible?

_____

_____

_____

5) What changes would you have to make?

_____

_____

_____

6) What changes would your partner have to make?

_____

_____

_____

Dealing Effectively with Needs Problems

A simple process that can help you and your partner deal more effectively with differences in your needs-sets include the following steps which can help you to understand each other's needs and learn to accept and embrace your differences.

1) UNDERSTAND YOUR OWN NEEDS

Partners who fight often fight over the same issues repeatedly. It is important to first understand what your needs are. Now that you have completed the assessment, what would you say are your greatest needs in your relationship?

_____

_____

_____

2) PERMIT YOURSELF TO EXPRESS YOUR NEEDS TO YOUR PARTNER

It is important to express your needs to your partner. Write how you could express these needs to your partner in the table that follows.

MY NEEDS	HOW I CAN EXPRESS THIS NEED TO MY PARTNER
Ex. I need him to WANT to know my feelings.	Ex. Since he doesn't always listen to me, I'll write him a note explaining how I prefer sharing my feelings with him more than with anyone else.

(Continued on the next page)

Dealing Effectively with Needs Problems *(continued)*

3) UNDERSTAND YOUR PARTNER'S NEEDS

It is also important to understand what your partner's needs are. Look back at the assessment you completed. What would you say are your partner's greatest needs in your relationship?

_____

_____

_____

4) LISTEN TO WHAT THE OTHER PERSON NEEDS

Think about the things that your partner says that should give you insights into your partner's needs. Write them below.

MY PARTNER'S NEEDS	HOW MY PARTNER TRIES TO EXPRESS THIS NEED
Ex. To spend an occasional evening with friends.	*Ex. Makes excuses about why his friends need him to come over.*

Relationship Needs

What have you learned (positive or negative) about your own needs?

_____

_____

_____

_____

_____

_____

_____

_____

_____

What surprised you of what you learned about yourself?

_____

_____

_____

_____

_____

_____

_____

_____

_____

Relationship Personality Quotations

☐ *You can't stop loving or wanting to love because when it's right, it's the best thing in the world. When you're in a relationship and it's good, even if nothing else in your life is right, you feel like your whole world is complete.*

~ Keith Sweat

☐ *Having someone wonder where you are when you don't come home at night is a very human need.*

~ Margaret Mead

Check one of the above quotes and journal your thoughts on how it applies, or does not apply, to you.

_____

_____

_____

_____

_____

_____

_____

_____

_____

_____

_____

_____

_____

_____

Negative Behaviors
That Often Lead to a Break-Up*

- **Criticism** – often appears as a complaint or blaming that attacks your partner's personality or character. Frequently begins with "You always" or "You never."

- **Defensiveness** – people reverse a situation to defend their innocence or to avoid taking responsibility for a problem.

- **Contempt** – criticism accompanied by hostility or disgust. Often involves sarcasm, mocking or name-calling.

- **Stonewalling** – listeners withdraw from a conversation and offer no physical or verbal cues that they are affected by what they hear.

- **Ignoring** – listeners refuse to pay attention to somebody or refuse to notice what somebody is saying.

* Adapted from Gottman, J.M., & Gottman. J.S. (2006).
10 lessons to transform your marriage. New York: Crown.

Factors Being Influenced by Compatibility

- Family

- Friends

- Health and Exercise

- Independence

- In-laws

- Intimacy

- Money and Time Management

- Life Style

- Smoking and Drinking Habits

- Travel

- Work – Leisure Balance

© 2010 WHOLE PERSON ASSOCIATES, 210 WEST MICHIGAN ST., DULUTH MN 55802-1908 ▪ 800-247-6789

SECTION IV:
Relationship Intimacy Scale

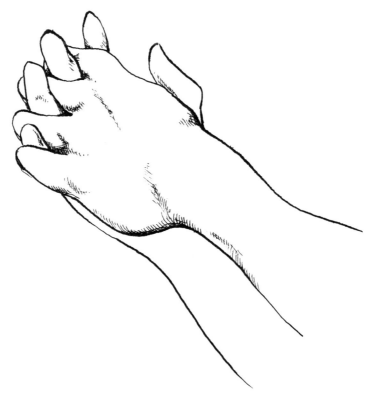

NAME _____ DATE _____

The relationship I will be referring to is with . . .

_____

Relationship Intimacy Scale Directions

Intimacy is a critical aspect in all relationships. The more intimate you and your partner are, the healthier and more satisfying your relationship will be. Most people equate intimacy with sex, but intimacy is truly much more. Intimacy can be seen in many aspects of the relationship that you have with your partner, including romance, compatibility, love and sex. The Relationship Intimacy Scale will help you examine the quality of the intimacy in your relationship with your partner.

This assessment contains 32 statements related to intimacy in your relationship with your partner. Read each of the statements and decide whether or not the statement describes you. If the statement is true, circle the number next to that item under the **TRUE** column. If the statement is false, circle the number next to that item under the **FALSE** column.

In the following example, the circled number under **FALSE** indicates the statement is not true of the person completing the inventory.

	TRUE	FALSE
(A) There is no longer fire and passion in our relationship	1	(2)

This is not a test and there are no right or wrong answers. Do not spend too much time thinking about your answers. Your initial response will likely be the most true for you. Be sure to respond to every statement.

(Turn to the next page and begin)

Relationship Intimacy Scale

	TRUE	FALSE
(A) There is no longer fire and passion in our relationship	1	2
(A) My partner and I do things that are fresh and exciting	2	1
(A) My partner and I often demonstrate our love for each other	2	1
(A) My partner and I no longer kiss and caress	1	2
(A) It is difficult to keep our romance alive	1	2
(A) I wish my partner would be more romantic	1	2
(A) My partner and I have less energy than we used to	2	1
(A) My partner and I often plan romantic dates and/or surprises	2	1
(B) My partner is my best friend	2	1
(B) I always have fun when I am with my partner	2	1
(B) I am spiritually incompatible with my partner	1	2
(B) I love spending time with my partner	2	1
(B) My partner and I both have similar values	2	1
(B) My partner and I have very different interests	1	2
(B) My partner and I do not have the same goals	1	2
(B) My partner and I have similar socio-economic backgrounds	2	1

(Continued on the next page)

(**Relationship Needs Scale** *continued*)

	TRUE	FALSE
(C) I often think about my partner when we are apart	2	1
(C) I would still be with the same partner if I had to do it over again	2	1
(C) I am not sure my partner appreciates me	1	2
(C) My partner and I often kiss affectionately	2	1
(C) I feel accepted by my partner	2	1
(C) We rarely tell each other "I love you"	1	2
(C) I find myself turning to others for support and comfort	1	2
(C) I am often bored in our relationship	1	2
(D) Our sexual life is boring	1	2
(D) I feel sexy when I am with my partner	2	1
(D) My partner and I find each other attractive	2	1
(D) My partner and I see each other as sexy	2	1
(D) One of us has too high a level of sexual expectations	1	2
(D) Our sexual life is still satisfying	2	1
(D) My partner and I have different sex drives	1	2
(D) We no longer please each other sexually	1	2

(Go to the Scoring Directions on the next page)

Relationship Intimacy Scale Scoring Directions

The Relationship Intimacy Scale is designed to measure the quality of your intimate relationships. To get your (A) Romance score, total the numbers you circled for statements marked (A), in the previous section. You will get a score from 8 to 16. Put that number on the line next to the (A) Romance Total scale that follows. Then, do the same for the other three scales: (B) Compatibility Total, (C) Love Total and (D) Sexual Total.

(A) ROMANCE TOTAL   = _____

(B) COMPATABILITY TOTAL = _____

(C) LOVE TOTAL   = _____

(D) SEXUAL TOTAL   = _____

Add the four scores you listed above to get your Overall Relationship Intimacy Total. Total scores on this assessment range from 32 to 64. Put your Overall Total score in the space below:

OVERALL INTIMATE RELATIONSHIP QUALITY TOTAL = _____

Profile Interpretation

INDIVIDUAL SCALE SCORES	RESULT	INDICATIONS
Scores from 8 to 10 or a total from 32 to 42	Low	You are probably experiencing a lack of intimacy in your relationship with your partner. You need to work on enhancing the intimacy in your relationship with the exercises that follow.
Scores from 11 to 13 or a total from 43 to 53	Moderate	You are probably experiencing some lack of intimacy in your relationship with your partner. By completing the exercises that follow, you can have even more intimacy in your relationship.
Scores from 14 to 16 or a total from 54 to 64	High	You are probably experiencing a great deal of intimacy in your relationship with your partner. The exercises that follow can help you enhance your intimate relationship even further.

(Go to the Scale Descriptions that follow)

Relationship Intimacy Scale Descriptions

SCALE A – Romance

People scoring low on this scale are experiencing a loss of romance in their relationship. They probably do not feel the passion that was once in the relationship, and are having trouble keeping the romance alive in their relationship. They no longer do the romantic things they did when they first started the relationship, and probably have a more difficult time showing affection and love for one another.

With effective relationships, partners find ways to keep the romance alive for themselves and their partners.

SCALE B – Compatibility

People scoring low on this scale sometimes are unable to connect with each other because they lack basic compatibility with one another. They probably have experienced a change in values, interests and goals, and no longer feel compatible.

With effective relationships, partners are able to connect with each other because they enjoy spending free time with each other, they have fun engaging in activities together, and they have the same basic needs, goals and dreams.

SCALE C – Love

People scoring low on this scale sometimes find themselves falling out of love with their partner. They think about how things used to be in the earlier stages of the relationship and how they would like a relationship to be. Sometimes couples begin to lose fondness and admiration for each other, stop telling their partner "I love you," and find themselves not being as comforting or supportive as they once were.

With effective relationships, partners exhibit a sense of excitement about their partner, maintain a sense of respect for their partner, and find themselves in as much love as the day they became partners, or more so.

SCALE D – Sexual

People scoring low on this scale tend to have less satisfying sex lives than they once had. They may feel that their sex life is boring or that their partner is no longer as attractive as they once were. They may have sexual expectations that are unrealistic and have a harder time pleasing, or being pleased by their partner.

With effective relationships, people accept changes in each other's sex drive and work to ensure that their sexual life is pleasurable for both people in the relationship.

Intimacy is an important part of any relationship and needs to be nurtured. Regardless of your scores on the assessment, the following exercises have been designed to help you enhance your intimate relationship with your partner. By completing the following exercises and activities, you will find that your intimate relationship with your partner will improve.

Romance

Early in most relationships, romance comes very easily and naturally, and it is exciting. As time goes on, couples become more familiar and comfortable with each other and romance often seems to come less naturally. Sometimes, romantic gestures even cease to occur. Think about if the romance between you and your partner has changed over time. In the table that follows, record in the upper block those romantic things you and your partner did when you first met. Then, in the lower block, list those romantic things you and your partner do now.

ROMANTIC THINGS WE DID WHEN WE MET
Ex. He brought me a flower almost every day.

ROMANTIC THINGS WE DO NOW
Ex. On our anniversary we go out on a special date.

Referring to the tables above, what are the differences in the romance in your life?

_____

_____

_____

_____

Has this changed your relationship? How?

_____

_____

_____

_____

Being Romantic

It is important to find ways to keep romance alive. Romance is an expression of love from one partner to another and can take many forms – words, gestures and actions. Think about the ways that you and your partner express your love to one another and complete the table that follows. In the middle column list the ways that you show love to your partner, and in the column on the far right, list the ways that your partner shows love to you.

HOW I CAN SHOW LOVE	HOW I SHOW I LOVE MY PARTNER	HOW MY PARTNER SHOWS LOVE
Words Say "I love you, E-mail "I'm thinking of you" Leave a note		
Gestures Hold hands Give a neck rub Smile in a special way		
Actions Present flowers Schedule a date Give a surprise		

In what ways can you be more romantic with your partner?

_____

_____

_____

In what ways would you like your partner to be romantic?

_____

_____

_____

Compatibility

Compatibility is about living in harmony with a partner as the dynamics of your relationship changes. Early in relationships, partners are probably very compatible. However, as they both grow as people, it affects the way in which they interact as partners. People who are compatible enjoy being with each other and having fun together, having similar interests and goals, and are good, if not best friends.

In what ways are you and your partner still compatible?

_____

_____

_____

In what ways are you and your partner not as compatible as you once were?

_____

_____

_____

In what ways do you still enjoy spending time with your partner?

_____

_____

_____

If you don't enjoy spending time with your partner, why not?

_____

_____

_____

When do you and your partner have fun together?

_____

_____

_____

What fun things did you and your partner used to do, that you no longer do? Why not?

_____

_____

_____

My Goals, Interests and Values

When goals and interests change in a relationship, partners often find themselves less compatible than they once were. In the tables that follow, identify the ways you and your partner's goals, interests and values have changed over time.

IMPORTANT FACTORS	AT THE BEGINNING OF OUR RELATIONSHIP	NOW
Goals Things you would like to accomplish		
Interests Things you enjoy doing		
Values Things important to you		

What differences stand out to you?

_____

_____

_____

My Partner's Goals, Interests and Values

IMPORTANT FACTORS	AT THE BEGINNING OF OUR RELATIONSHIP	NOW
Goals Things your partner would like to accomplish		
Interests Things your partner enjoys doing		
Values Things important to your partner		

What differences stand out to you?

_____

_____

_____

Love

Partners sometimes reach a stage when they feel too busy or tired to relate effectively to one another. Nothing may be wrong, but the relationship does not seem to feel right. Sometimes partners may feel bored or so comfortable that they forget how much they really love each other. We often forget how much we appreciate our partners and often take them for granted. Complete the following love exercises:

What do you appreciate about your partner?

_____

_____

_____

What do you think your partner appreciates about you?

_____

_____

_____

How can you better express your affection for your partner?

_____

_____

_____

How can your partner better express affection for you?

_____

_____

_____

How do you support your partner?

_____

_____

_____

(Continued on the next page)

Love (continued)

How does your partner support you?

_____

_____

_____

How do you comfort your partner?

_____

_____

_____

How does your partner comfort you?

_____

_____

_____

What weaknesses of your partner do you accept?

_____

_____

_____

What weaknesses of yours does your partner accept?

_____

_____

_____

How can you make more time for love to have "meaningful" talks, go to dinner for date night, etc.?

_____

_____

_____

Taking for Granted

As relationships develop, partners often become more comfortable with one another and begin to take the other for granted.

Being taken for granted includes such things as:

- **Getting used to and beginning to expect that the partner will continue to do all of the wonderful things the partner has been doing.**
- **Expecting someone or something to be available all of the time**
- **Forgetting to appreciate your partner**
- **Failing to acknowledge the special things your partner does for or with you**

Think about your current relationship and answer the following questions:

In what ways do you take your partner for granted?

_____

_____

_____

In what ways does your partner take you for granted?

_____

_____

_____

Taking For Granted Quotations

☐ *When it comes to life the critical thing is whether you take things for granted or take them with gratitude.* ~ **G. K. Chesterton**

☐ *Life is a gift. Never take it for granted.* ~ **Sasha Azevedo**

☐ *Being taken for granted can be a compliment. It means you've become a comfortable, trusted element in another person's life.* ~ **Dr. Joyce Brothers**

Check off which of these quotes above resonate with you. Why?

_____

_____

_____

_____

Boring . . .

If you and/or your partner have become bored in your relationship, how do you think this came about?

REASONS I HAVE BECOME BORED IN MY RELATIONSHIP
Ex: My partner works too much. We don't have time to spend together, so I do many things by myself. We do not seem to be interested in what the other is doing.

REASONS MY PARTNER HAS BECOME BORED IN OUR RELATIONSHIP
Ex: We have moved closer to my parents since they have gotten older. I have been spending more time with my family and I like talking about them a lot.

Sexual Drive

The sexual drive of partners in a relationship can change because of stress, illness, medication, age, boredom, fatigue, indifference and/or lack of variety or excitement.

How would you describe your sex drive?

_____

_____

_____

How would you describe your partner's sex drive?

_____

_____

_____

In what ways do you find your partner sexy? Not sexy?

_____

_____

_____

In what ways do you try to maintain your sex-appeal for your partner? How about your partner?

_____

_____

_____

Describe your feelings after sex when you first started a relationship with your partner.

_____

_____

_____

Describe your feelings after sex in your current relationship with your partner.

_____

_____

_____

Sexual Life

In the following table, write your thoughts and feelings about your sexual life with your partner.

ISSUES RELATED TO SEX	MY THOUGHTS AND FEELINGS
The frequency of our lovemaking	
The changes in my sex drive	
The changes in my partner's sex drive	
The changes in my sex technique	
The changes in my partner's sex technique	
Sexual variety in our lovemaking	
Sexual performance of my partner	
My own sexual performance	

What did you learn about yourself?

_____

_____

_____

What did you learn about your partner?

_____

_____

_____

I Have Learned . . .

In terms of the intimacy issues surrounding your relationship, what have you learned most about yourself?

_____

_____

_____

_____

_____

What have you learned most about your partner?

_____

_____

_____

_____

_____

What will you do to make the relationship with your partner more intimate?
(think in terms of romance, compatibility, love, and sex)

_____

_____

_____

_____

_____

_____

_____

Relationship Intimacy Quotations

☐ *Remember, we all stumble, every one of us. That's why it's a comfort to go hand in hand.*
~ Emily Kimbrough

☐ *In the coldest February, as in every other month in every other year, the best thing to hold on to in this world is each other.*
~ Linda Ellerbee

Check one of the above quotes and journal your thoughts on how it applies to you.

_____

_____

_____

_____

_____

_____

_____

_____

_____

_____

_____

_____

_____

_____

_____

_____

Ways of Keeping Romance in Your Relationship

- Know and understand what your partner considers romantic . . . and do it!

- Be affectionate in public (in an appropriate way)

- Say "I love you" often

- Repeat the romantic gestures you did in the beginning of your relationship

- Show the kind of physical affection your partner enjoys (give your partner a massage, put your arm around your partner, hold your partner's hand when walking outdoors, cook a special dinner for your partner, give your partner an "I love you present" (flowers, candy, tickets to a ball game, etc.)

Decreasing Intimacy

- You don't care what's happening in your partner's life

- You rarely say "I love you"

- You do not look forward to spending time together

- You stop talking to your partner about important or unimportant issues

- You touch your partner less

- You find excuses to avoid making love

- You find excuses to spend more time alone

- You stay out of the house more often and for longer periods of time

- You no longer try to please your partner

SECTION V:
Relationship Conflicts Scale

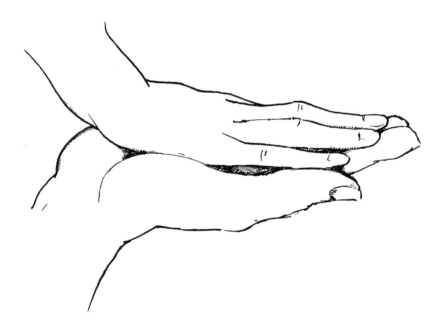

NAME _____ DATE _____

The relationship I will be referring to is with . . .

_____

Relationship Conflicts Scale Directions

In relationships, people bring a variety of personality traits, values, opinions, ways of expressing their feelings and ways of behaving. It is no wonder that partners in any relationship eventually must cope with a variety of relationship issues that will cause conflict. The Relationship Conflicts Scale can help you to identify the primary issues that cause the most conflict between you and your partner. If a section does not apply to you and your partner (Children Scale for example), just skip that section and move to the next section.

The following assessment contains 40 statements. Use the choices listed below. Read each of the statements and circle the number to the right that best describes how much you value each statement.

Circle **4** if the statement is **Very True** for you
Circle **3** if the statement is **Somewhat True** for you
Circle **2** if the statement is **A Little True** for you
Circle **1** if the statement is **Not True** for you

In the following example, the circled **3** indicates that the statement is **Somewhat True** for the person completing the scale.

When it comes to honesty and trust, my partner and I argue about . . .

how loyal we are to each other   4   (3)   2   1

This is not a test and there are no right or wrong answers. Do not spend too much time thinking about your answers. Your initial response will likely be the most true for you. Be sure to respond to every statement.

(Turn to the next page and begin)

Relationship Conflicts Scale

Circle **4** if the statement is **Very True** for you
Circle **3** if the statement is **Somewhat True** for you
Circle **2** if the statement is **A Little True** for you
Circle **1** if the statement is **Not True** for you

HONESTY AND TRUST

When it comes to honesty and trust, my partner and I argue about . . .

how loyal we are to each other	4	3	2	1
how much we can be trusted and believed	4	3	2	1
how honest we are about personal feelings	4	3	2	1
how much we can depend on each other	4	3	2	1
how certain it is that we would never cheat on each other	4	3	2	1

HONESTY AND TRUST TOTAL _____

HOUSEHOLD WORKLOAD

When it comes to household workload, my partner and I argue about . . .

who does or arranges the home repairs	4	3	2	1
who makes or should be making entertainment arrangements	4	3	2	1
who prepares or should prepare most of the meals	4	3	2	1
who does or should do the laundry	4	3	2	1
who does or should do most of the grocery shopping	4	3	2	1

HOUSEHOLD WORKLOAD TOTAL _____

WORK-RELATIONSHIP BALANCE

When it comes to balancing work and relationship, my partner and I argue about . . .

how much time we spend at work	4	3	2	1
how much time we take off to relax	4	3	2	1
how many social and leisure activities we pass up	4	3	2	1
how many trips and vacations to take and where to go	4	3	2	1
how much time we spend together	4	3	2	1

WORK-RELATIONSHIP BALANCE TOTAL _____

(Continued on the next page)

(**Relationship Conflicts Scale** *continued*)

Circle **4** if the statement is **Very True** for you
Circle **3** if the statement is **Somewhat True** for you
Circle **2** if the statement is **A Little True** for you
Circle **1** if the statement is **Not True** for you

MONEY MANAGEMENT

When it comes to managing money, my partner and I argue about . . .

how much to save	4	3	2	1
how much to spend	4	3	2	1
how to invest our money	4	3	2	1
how to budget our money	4	3	2	1
who writes the checks and balances the checkbook	4	3	2	1

MONEY MANAGEMENT TOTAL _____

EXTENDED FAMILIES

When it comes to our extended families, my partner and I argue about . . .

how accepted we are by each other's family	4	3	2	1
how important are our families-of-origin	4	3	2	1
how much time to spend with each of our families	4	3	2	1
how much we should please our families-of-origin	4	3	2	1
how intrusive are our families-of-origin	4	3	2	1

EXTENDED FAMILIES TOTAL _____

CHILDREN

When it comes to raising children, my partner and I argue about . . .

how to handle children problems	4	3	2	1
who takes the children to practices and events	4	3	2	1
how to discipline our children	4	3	2	1
who helps with school homework	4	3	2	1
what values to instill in our children	4	3	2	1

CHILDREN TOTAL _____

(Continued on the next page)

(Relationship Conflicts Scale *continued*)

Circle **4** if the statement is **Very True** for you
Circle **3** if the statement is **Somewhat True** for you
Circle **2** if the statement is **A Little True** for you
Circle **1** if the statement is **Not True** for you

RELIGION AND SPIRITUALITY

When it comes to religion and spirituality, my partner and I argue about . . .

our religious or spiritual beliefs and values	4	3	2	1
what house of worship to attend and how often	4	3	2	1
religious and spiritual issues	4	3	2	1
our religious identity	4	3	2	1
how much money to contribute	4	3	2	1

RELIGION AND SPIRITUALITY TOTAL _____

INTIMACY

When it comes to intimacy, my partner and I argue about . . .

who initiates sex most of the time	4	3	2	1
who is responsible for birth control	4	3	2	1
how often we are intimate	4	3	2	1
how to be intimate	4	3	2	1
how to show our love for each other	4	3	2	1

INTIMACY TOTAL _____

(Go to the Scoring Directions on the next page)

Relationship Conflicts Scale Scoring Directions

Cooperative partners work together so they can avoid conflicts. However, conflicts can occur in a wide variety of different areas. For each of the eight sections on the previous pages, count the scores you circled. Put that total on the line marked TOTAL at the end of each section.

Then, transfer your totals to the spaces below:

HONESTY AND TRUST TOTAL = _____

HOUSEHOLD WORKLOAD TOTAL = _____

WORK-RELATIONSHIP BALANCE TOTAL = _____

MONEY MANAGEMENT TOTAL = _____

EXTENDED FAMILIES TOTAL = _____

CHILDREN TOTAL = _____

RELIGION AND SPIRITUALITY TOTAL = _____

INTIMACY TOTAL = _____

Profile Interpretation

TOTAL INDIVIDUAL SCALE SCORES	RESULT	INDICATIONS
Scores from 16 to 20	High	You and your partner are experiencing a great deal of conflict in this area, which may be leading to many arguments.
Scores from 10 to 15	Moderate	You and your partner are experiencing some conflict in this area, which may be leading to some arguments.
Scores from 5 to 9	Low	You and your partner are experiencing little conflict in this area.

For scales which you scored in the **Moderate** or **High** range, find the descriptions on the pages that follow. Then, read the description and complete the exercises that are included. No matter how you scored, low, moderate or high, you will benefit from these exercises.

Honesty and Trust

People with a high score on this scale tend to argue with their partners about honesty and trust issues. What changes would you like to see in how you and your partner are honest with and trustful of each other?

AREAS OF CONFLICT	OUR CURRENT SITUATION	THE IDEAL SITUATION
Loyalty	*Ex: My partner complains about me to friends and family.*	*Ex: My partner would tell me what he's upset about but no one else.*
Trustworthiness		
Honesty		
Dependability		
Fidelity		
Other		

Household Workload

People with a high score on this scale tend to argue with their partners about distribution of the household workload. What changes would you like to see in how you and your partner share the workload?

AREAS OF CONFLICT	OUR CURRENT SITUATION	THE IDEAL SITUATION
Home Repairs	*Ex: My partner expects me to stay home from work to wait for the repair man implying that my job is not as important.*	*Ex: Take turns so each one shares the responsibility.*
Arrangements		
Meals		
Laundry		
Grocery shopping		
Other		

Work-Relationship Balance

People with a high score on this scale tend to argue with their partners about their ability to balance work and relationship. What changes would you like to see in how you and your partner balance work and your relationship?

AREAS OF CONFLICT	OUR CURRENT SITUATION	THE IDEAL SITUATION
Time at work	*Ex: My partner works for herself and puts in 12 hours a day, 6 days a week.*	*Ex: Either coming home for dinner and going back to work or limiting hours.*
Time off		
Missing activities for work		
Vacations		
How much time to spend together		
Other		

Money Management

People with a high score on this scale tend to argue with their partners about managing money. What changes would you like to see in how you and your partner manage money?

AREAS OF CONFLICT	OUR CURRENT SITUATION	THE IDEAL SITUATION
How much to save	*Ex: My partner spends every penny we make.*	*Ex: We decide on a fixed amount and save it from every paycheck, no matter what!*
Where to keep it		
Where to invest it		
How to spend it		
Balancing checkbook		
Other		

Extended Families

People with a high score on this scale tend to argue with their partners about their extended families. What changes would you like to see in how you and your partner view your extended families?

AREAS OF CONFLICT	OUR CURRENT SITUATION	THE IDEAL SITUATION
Acceptance of other's family	*Ex: My partner's family has come to accept me but do not include me or go out of their way for me.*	*Ex: I want to feel like one of their own.*
Time spent		
Involvement and say they should have		
Attempts to please them		
Intruding in our lives		
Other		

Children

People with a high score on this scale tend to argue with their partners about raising their children. What changes would you like to see in how you and your partner share responsibilities with your children?

AREAS OF CONFLICT	OUR CURRENT SITUATION	THE IDEAL SITUATION
Handling problems	*Ex: My partner tells the kids that I'll take care of the problem when I get home and then doesn't approve of the way I handle it.*	*Ex: We are each handling situations equally or work together. We decide ahead of time the way to handle each situation.*
Child care		
Daily discipline and/or methods of discipline		
Homework		
Time spent		
Other		

Religion and Spirituality

People with a high score on this scale tend to argue with their partners about religion and spirituality issues. What changes would you like to see in how you and your partner view and participate with religion and spirituality?

AREAS OF CONFLICT	OUR CURRENT SITUATION	THE IDEAL SITUATION
Worship	Ex: If I want to go to a house of worship, I go without my partner.	Ex: Once in a while my partner could go with me, choosing where we attend.
Beliefs and/or values		
Issues		
Identity		
How much money and/or time to contribute		
Other		

Intimacy

People with a high score on this scale tend to argue with their partners about issues related to intimacy and/or sex. What changes would you like to see in how you and your partner approach intimacy and/or sex?

AREAS OF CONFLICT	OUR CURRENT SITUATION	THE IDEAL SITUATION
Initiating intimacy or sex	*Ex: It is always me initiating sex or even a hug. I am often refused.*	*Ex: If my partner initiated it sometimes I wouldn't mind being refused at times.*
Responsibility for birth control		
How often?		
How?		
Using sex to meet other needs		
How we show our love for each other		

Negotiation Steps

People in healthy relationships negotiate with their partners rather than argue and fight. Negotiation is a type of communication you can use to get what you want or need, compromising at times, and without manipulation or making your partner angry.

Steps to Successful Negotiating

1) Prepare for the negotiation

The first step is to pose the problem in a non-confrontational manner. Remember that the result should be something that is beneficial to both you and your partner. Be careful to avoid trying to win, blaming, overwhelming or venting your anger. The situation:

James thinks that his partner Karen works too much and leaves him with a heavy family workload.

2) Describe the situation to your partner – Use I-Messages

Try to avoid being too emotional, negative or argumentative.

James: *"I was hoping that you could work a little less than you do now. When you work so much, I get stuck doing most of the household chores and taking care of the children. I work too, but I try and keep my work hours to about forty a week. Right now you are working a lot more than that."*

Karen: *"Yes, I am working on a big project and I hope to get back to a normal work schedule soon."*

3) Share feelings – Use I-Messages

Share your feelings about the situation.

James: *"I know you are and I appreciate how hard you work. However, I am getting frustrated and I feel a little taken advantage of by you. I feel like you think your job is more important than mine."*

Karen: *"I did not realize how much I was working. I think that your job is as important as mine. I don't want to take advantage of you."*

4) Share what you and your partner want in the situation – Use I-Messages

Share what you want in the situation and then ask your partner the same question.

James: *"I was hoping that you could cut back your hours, take some vacation time every now and then, and help out a little more with the children."*

Karen: *"I will try to do that, and perhaps you could continue to help with meals and laundry."*

5) Identify possible solutions

Identify several possible solutions.

James could possibly help Karen in some way with her workload.
Karen could reduce her work hours or work some from home if possible.
James or Karen could quit his/her job.
James and Karen could work collaboratively on the weekends and evenings.

6) Choose

Choose the best solution for both of you. Karen would work less. She also would be more assertive at work, saying "no" to taking on too many projects and James could continue to help more with other responsibilities.

Negotiation Steps – You Try!

Remember that most partners in a relationship argue. Most important is to negotiate for what you want, while keeping in mind your partner's wants and needs. Remember that the end result is a win-win solution for both you and your partner. Now you try it. Think about a situation that you would like to change. Use one of the categories of the assessment, or another one if you like.

1) Prepare for the negotiation.

The first step is to pose the problem in a non-confrontational manner. Remember that the result should be something that is good for both you and your partner. Be careful to avoid trying to win, blame, overwhelm, or vent your anger. What is the situation?

_____

_____

2) Describe the situation to your partner. – Use I-Messages.

Try not to be emotional, negative or argumentative.

_____

_____

3) Share your feelings about the situation. – Use I-Messages.

_____

_____

4) Share what you and your partner want in the situation. – Use I-Messages.

_____

_____

5) Identify possible solutions.

_____

_____

_____

_____

_____

6) Choose the best solution for both of you.

_____

_____

Negotiating

Which conflict areas are the hardest for you to negotiate and overcome? Why is that?

_____

_____

_____

_____

_____

Which conflict areas are the hardest for your partner to negotiate and overcome? Why is that?

_____

_____

_____

_____

_____

How will you introduce the idea of negotiating to your partner?

_____

_____

_____

_____

_____

What do you project the response to be? Why?

_____

_____

_____

_____

_____

Relationship Quotations

☐ *Health is the greatest gift, contentment the greatest wealth, faithfulness the best relationship.*

~ Buddha

☐ *Trouble is part of your life, and if you don't share it, you don't give the person who loves you enough chance to love you enough.*

~ Dinah Shore

Check one of the above quotes and journal your thoughts on how it applies, or does not apply, to you.

_____

_____

_____

_____

_____

_____

_____

_____

_____

_____

_____

_____

_____

_____

_____

_____

Important Points to Remember When Negotiating

- Do not blame your partner for what is happening

- Be careful to avoid threatening, belittling, criticizing or causing your partner to feel guilty

- Try to put yourself in your partner's shoes

- Listen actively to the messages behind the words of your partner

- Keep remembering (and even restating) that the goal is a fair, mutually agreed upon solution that is good for both of you

- Compromise is an ultimate goal for negotiating any conflict or situation

Principles of Negotiation*

Negotiation involves two parties with important, legitimate, but opposing interests.

- Realize that conflict is inevitable

- Use I-Messages

- Resist name calling, threats or anger

- Separate feelings from the issue

- Focus on interests, not positions

- Seek mutually agreeable options

- Show persistence

- Maintain flexibility

*Adapted from McKay, M., Fanning, P., & Paleg, K. (1994). *Couple Skills*. Oakland, CA: New Harbinger

122

wholeperson

Whole Person Associates is the leading publisher of training resources for professionals who empower people to create and maintain healthy lifestyles. Our creative resources will help you work effectively with your clients in the areas of stress management, wellness promotion, mental health and life skills.

Please visit us at our web site: www.wholeperson.com. You can check out our entire line of products, place an order, request our print catalog, and sign up for our monthly special notifications.

Whole Person Associates
210 W Michigan
Duluth MN 55802
800-247-6789